Kingston Lacy
Garden and Park

Dorset

A Perfectly Ordered Paradise

William John Bankes, who introduced the Egyptian obelisk and the sculpture on the South Lawn

Henrietta Bankes, who ran the Kingston Lacy after the early death of her husband in 1904

(*Opposite*) The Parterre still has its Edwardian formal planting devised by Henrietta Bankes and her head gardener

The Kingston Lacy gardens reached their grandest heights in the Edwardian era, during the reign of the formidable Henrietta Bankes and her head gardener, Mr Hill. She laid out the Parterre (4) and the Sunken Garden (7) with their formal topiary and brashly coloured bedding plants. In the summer, she would invite friends for leisurely games of tennis on the South Lawn (3), followed by tea, which a footman would carry down the terrace steps on a heavily laden silver tray at 5 o'clock. Her daughter, Viola, remembered being taken for walks through the flower-filled woods by the nurserymaid with her sister Daphne and brother Ralph (then still in his pram), while their nanny walked majestically behind: 'The park and the garden were meticulously tended. To Daphne, Ralph and me, not even realising how lucky we were, as long as we obeyed the rules, it was a perfectly ordered Paradise.'

But the garden and park have a much longer history, of which you can catch glimpses everywhere. The Lime Walk (12) still contains trees planted by Sir Ralph Bankes in the 1660s to adorn the landscape around his new house. The open parkland dates mostly from the 18th century. In the 1830s and '40s William John Bankes introduced a touch of the exotic to the South Lawn, with Italian sculpture and an ancient Egyptian obelisk acquired on his Mediterranean travels.

By the time Ralph Bankes generously bequeathed Kingston Lacy and its huge estate to the National Trust in 1981, the gardens were in decline. It has taken much effort and imagination to return them to their Edwardian heyday. Appropriate new attractions are being added every year, and – as in every garden – more still remains to be done.

Key dates

1229	John de Lacy, 1st Earl of Lincoln granted manor of Kingston
1349	Kingston Lacy becomes part of the royal Duchy of Lancaster
by 1493	Medieval manor house in ruins
1636	Sir John Bankes buys the estate
1665	Sir Ralph Bankes builds the new house
1835	Sir Charles Barry remodels the house for William John Bankes
c.1900	Henrietta Bankes lays out the garden
1981	Ralph Bankes bequeaths the estate to the National Trust
1990	Storm damages the park

Henrietta Bankes in the park with her three children

The Park

The Woodland Walk in spring. In August 1943 a 1,314-bed American hospital was built in the east park, which treated thousands of patients following the D-Day landings

On 25 January 1990, a storm devastated the park. Tangled in the roots of a tree that fell in the northern park were fragments of medieval pottery and roof tiles. These revealed the site of the long-lost manor house owned in the mid-13th century by the de Lacy family, who gave their name to the estate. By 1252 Kingston Lacy was attracting royalty: 756 gallons of wine were ordered to celebrate Henry III's visit that year, and the deer-park would have provided venison, rabbits and hares for the royal table. Between 1362 and 1399 Kingston Lacy belonged to Edward III's son, John of Gaunt, who spent several Christmases here, cutting down oak trees in the park as gifts for local retainers. The medieval manor house was in ruins by the 1490s, but the park survived its disappearance, and the enclosure of the surrounding farmland.

The park was enlarged to its present 161 hectares (399 acres) following the Enclosure Act of 1784, when the hamlet of Kingston was swept away and open parkland was created. The present appearance of the park reflects successive campaigns of planting in the 19th century, when beeches, Spanish Chestnuts, planes and Portugal Laurel were introduced in small groups rather than the more conventional clumps. However, the park is now barer than intended, following the 1990 storm, which brought down over 1,000 trees. The Trust is re-establishing the vital shelter belt around the park and maintaining the 19th-century woodlands within the park by replacing individual trees when they reach the end of their lives. It has also created new woodland walks through the shelter belt, to link the park and garden with the car-park.

The North Devon cattle, which are such an attractive feature of the park, were introduced by Walter Ralph Bankes in the late 19th century. They continue to be reared for beef, which is sold through a local butcher.

In January 1990 a storm brought down over 1,000 trees in the park

The Garden

The Spoon Walk

The rose 'Amber Queen' fills the bed at the end of the South Terrace

The garden of the medieval manor house was probably more useful than ornamental. In 1380 it was producing pears, grapes, leeks, garlic and parsley.

In the 1660s Sir Ralph Bankes laid out formal gardens around his new house, with tree-lined avenues radiating from the main fronts. They were still in place in 1775, when William Woodward made a survey of the estate. However, ten years later, they were swept away, to be replaced by a landscape park with lawns sweeping right up to the house in the then-fashionable style of 'Capability' Brown. Formality returned in 1835, as a new terrace was built against William John Bankes's remodelled Kingston Lacy.

Walter Ralph Bankes and his wife Henrietta gave the garden its present shape in the early 1900s. The Kitchen Garden also dates from this period. Placed outside the boundary of the park, it contained a formal area with lawn, summer-house and herbaceous borders. Glasshouses produced dessert grapes and peaches for the table, and a cutting border provided flowers to decorate the house and for sale in Wimborne market. Viola Bankes remembers 'fragile, exotic orchids, leafy bougainvilia and soft blue, phlox-like plumbago, yellow guavas and melons trained to grow upright on the walls. There were all kinds of berries in mouth-watering profusion, even huge, sweet strawberries in February, as well as both red and white raspberries, red and green gooseberries and purple loganberries.'

Like many kitchen gardens in the mid-20th century, it fell into decay. Only one glasshouse remains, and the site is now let to a grower of bonsai trees. By the time Kingston Lacy was given to the National Trust in 1981, the rest of the garden was in an equally dilapidated state. Since the 1980s the Trust has undertaken a comprehensive restoration programme, following the Edwardian garden plans made by Henrietta Bankes. The final phase of the work will focus on the Lady Walk and Tea Garden, which lie in the woodland to the south of the formal gardens.

Hyde azaleas on the Spoon Walk

The South Lawn and Terrace in 1868, after William John Bankes had remodelled the house

Tour of the Garden

The South Terrace

A detail from one of the Venetian well-heads on the South Terrace

The Rose Garden (1)

This garden was laid out about 1882, at the same time as the building of the stables, in what was originally a service area next to the 18th-century kitchen and laundry. The central rotunda was used for exercising the horses.

The circular beds were once planted with pampas grass, but are now filled with roses to provide summer interest for visitors. The varieties chosen include the pink 'Bonica', mauve 'Cardinal Hume' and white 'Anne Zinkiesen', together with the low spreading *Rosa* 'Nozomi'. In spring, these beds are carpeted with *Scilla siberica* 'Spring Beauty'.

The South Terrace (2)

This was the creation of William John Bankes between 1835 and 1841. He also collected or commissioned the garden sculpture and ornaments here, and had green-painted wooden boxes made to protect them from winter frosts – a practice continued by the National Trust. Clipped bay trees (*Laurus nobilis*) sit in marble tubs, which were carved for Bankes in Verona in the form of traditional Italian well-heads. Some are supported on tortoises – a typically quirky Bankes touch. The *tazza*, or broad vase, contains cordylines.

To provide shade in this sunny spot, a striped awning was slung on bronze rings fixed to the side of the house, supported by poles set into the bronze 'vases' on the balustrade. The terrace planting follows Henrietta Bankes's scheme of the early 1900s: box-edged beds filled with dark red 'Vulcan' wallflowers in spring, and the bright red geranium 'Paul Crampel' in summer. Yew hedges close off both ends of the terrace; at the west end, they form a rectangular enclosure, within which is a bed of the rose 'Amber Queen' edged by another box hedge.

The South Lawn (3)

The dominating, central feature is an Egyptian obelisk. William John Bankes first saw it in 1815 at the Temple of Isis on the island of Philae during his pioneering expedition up the River Nile. He did not finally re-erect it here until 1839 and only after numerous mishaps on the voyage back to Britain. The Duke of Wellington, who was a friend of Bankes, laid the foundation stone, and it took a team of nineteen horses to haul the obelisk upright.

The sarcophagus was a gift to Bankes from the British Consul in Egypt in 1822.

The cannons point symbolically in the direction of Charborough Park, the home of the Drax family, with whom the Bankeses had a dispute dating back to the siege of Corfe Castle during the Civil War. The Draxes return the compliment by pointing another set of cannons at Kingston Lacy.

To the south, the views extend over the ha-ha (or concealed ditch) to the open parkland beyond. Holm oaks and a Cedar of Lebanon line the west side of the lawn, while to the east, a box hedge encloses the Fernery (5), behind which are Syringas, Forsythia and Viburnum, underplanted with Hellebores and Euphorbia.

Pink 'Bonica' roses fill the circular beds in front of the Stables

The Egyptian obelisk on the South Lawn

(*Left*) Curving steps lead down from the South Terrace to the South Lawn

The curling tendrils
of young ferns

The Fernery

(*Opposite*) The Parterre

The Parterre (4)

Although this garden, which lies to the east of the house, is not open to visitors, you can get a good view of it from the South Terrace.

Barry had proposed a formal flower garden for this area, which you would have entered directly from the loggia on the main stairs, but his idea was not adopted. It was not until 1899 that the Salisbury diocesan architect C.E. Ponting laid out the present parterre as a formal Dutch garden. The topiary 'skittles' and balls of Golden Yew were added in 1912.

The planting is again in the spirit of Henrietta Bankes's scheme: Snow-in-Summer (*Cerastium tomentosum*) edges beds of 'Vulcan' and Golden Monarch'

wall flowers and Forget-me-nots in spring, followed by salmon pink non-stop begonias and blue heliotrope 'Princess Marina'.

Beyond the Parterre is another lawn, alongside which is a shrub border that is at its best in spring, when the Magnolias and Forsythias come into flower. It is known affectionately as 'Granny Bankes's Garden' after Henrietta Bankes, who created it and could look down on it from her dressing-room window.

Stretching away to the east from this lawn is the Cedar Avenue (16), which was planted in 1835. The avenue suffered considerable damage in the 1990 gale, but replacement trees are gradually filling the gaps.

The Fernery (5)

The Victorians were fascinated by ferns. The Fernery, which was completed by 1900, is a rare surviving example of a garden area designed expressly to display ferns. It is a shady maze of narrow paths that thread between the low dry-stone walls which enclose the raised beds. Ferns need shade and moisture – the yews and the small pond with a fountain provide them. Over twenty varieties are grown here, and the fern theme is picked up in the decoration of the cast-iron garden seats.

In spring the Fernery is carpeted with snowdrops, followed by the Wood Anemone (*Anemone nemorosa*), of which Kingston Lacy has the National Collection. The climbing *Hydrangea petiolaris* grows over the wall that encloses the east side of the Fernery. The fig tree against the wall outside began life inside a lean-to glasshouse that has long since disappeared.

The Sunken Garden

The Cedar Walk (6)

This runs south from the South Terrace, dividing the Fernery from the Sunken Garden.

The Sunken Garden (7)

The layout and planting are as proposed by the garden designer William Goldring of Kew, who described his plans in letters to Walter Ralph Bankes in 1899–1904. The four lead statues date from the early 20th century, and originally stood in the Kitchen Garden.

The spring bedding is the pink Hyacinth 'Lady Derby', followed in summer by begonias – an edging of 'Olympic White' infilled with 'Olympic Pink'. The two oval beds are carpeted with *Scilla siberica* 'Spring Beauty' in spring. The main planting is of *Fuchsia* 'Madame Cornelissen', edged with the hardy variety 'Tom Thumb'. The central bed has pampas grass surrounded by Rodgersias.

The Blind Wood (8)

You enter the Blind Wood from behind a fern-leaved beech (*Fagus sylvatica* var. *heterophylla* 'Aspleniifolia') on the South Lawn. Because of the dense evergreen planting around the wood, there are no views either in or out – hence its name. The Edwardian scheme created bold contrasts of foliage colour: red *Berberis* × *ottawensis purpurea* and yellow *Taxus baccata* 'Elegantissima' against dark green Portugal Laurel. In spring the blossoming prunus trees and the underplanting of *Pulmonaria* varieties in full flower are the chief interest. In autumn the acers come into their own, providing another bold colour combination with the shrubs below them.

A statue in the Sunken Garden

The Blind Wood walk continues past the Victoria Monument, which Walter Ralph Bankes erected in 1887 on his 34th birthday to celebrate the Queen's Golden Jubilee. Around the monument are four Lucombe oaks (*Quercus* × *hispanica* 'Lucombeana').

The Cricket Walk (9)

This once led to an area of the park that served as the family cricket pitch. The National Trust has introduced groups of cistus and hydrangea with hardy geraniums and Japanese anemones. Behind these are clumps of Portugal Laurel, *Viburnum tinus*, pampas grass and bamboo.

The Lady Walk (10)

This led to the former Kitchen Garden, which was first set out about 1900. The walk passes through woodland between banks of ornamental shrubs, acers, bamboo and flowering cherry trees. This area still awaits restoration.

The Japanese Tea Garden (11)

The Trust also plans to restore the Tea Garden, which is in a clearing cut into the rising ground. The Tea Garden was enclosed by ornamental iron railings and comprised a summer-house, a central bed of azaleas edged with hostas, and a perimeter planting of bamboo (a large clump of which still survives), and shrubs such as philadelphus.

Portugal Laurels top the bank at the back of the garden with ferns on the steep slope.

Snowdrops cover the banks of the Lady Walk in early spring

The Lime Walk with its spring carpet of bluebells

The Lime Walk (12)

This avenue of native limes still contains trees planted as long ago as 1668. In 1875 Walter Ralph Bankes extended the walk up to the park side of the Nursery Wood. Lime trees throw out many shoots, which are pruned back every year, giving the older trees a characteristically barrel-shaped bole. The Lime Walk is under-planted with snowdrops, daffodils and bluebells.

The Nursery Wood (13) and Spoon Walk (14)

In the 17th century, the Nursery Wood was used to grow the trees required for planting out in the park. The traditional broad-leaved species were supplemented with a collection of conifers in the 19th century.

In 1905 the Spoon Walk was laid out round the perimeter of the Nursery Wood (the bowl of a spoon), as an extension of the Lime Walk (the handle of the spoon). In 1996 an area of lime-free greensand was planted with over 500 mature rhododendrons, azaleas and camellias. They were the gift of Rosemary Legrand, whose father, George Hyde, had raised many hybrids of these plants. He sold his first collection of deciduous azaleas (now known as the Solent Series) to Edmund de Rothschild of Exbury Garden in Hampshire, which is world-famous for its rhododendrons. Rosemary Legrand's gift includes her father's collection of rhododendrons with Shakespearean connections: the red 'Falstaff', yellow 'Prospero', lilac 'Verona' and white 'Midsummer Night's Dream'. She hopes to be able to add to the collection. From the Spoon Walk a gate leads into the Cedar Avenue, from where you have a good view of the east front of the house. The planting here is *Rhododendron yakushimanum*, including various hybrids and the three pure white parent plants George Hyde used for hybridising. In spring this is a sea of snowdrops, daffodils and fritillaries, while the deciduous azaleas, acers and *Ginkgo biloba* provide autumn colour.

The Laurel Walk (15)

It runs parallel to the Lime Walk and is lined with Portugal Laurel. The Trust has introduced camellias, which were part of the 1996 gift of rhododendrons and azaleas to be seen on the Spoon Walk.

Rhododendron 'Susan' in the Nursery Wood

(*Right*) The Nursery Wood in early spring

(*Opposite*) The Spoon Walk

The Cedar Avenue (16)

Many of the Cedars of Lebanon were planted by famous visitors, including the Duke of Wellington (1827), the Kaiser (1907; this has a seat round it) and Prince Charles (1996). They all used the same silver spade.

The sundial is inscribed, 'Life is short – Time is swift – Much is to be done'. The island bed nearby contains the Royal Fern *Osmunda regalis*, which was chosen for its autumn colour.

The shrubbery on the east side of the walk features white spring-flowering shrubs, such as *Deutzia*, *Exochorda* and *Viburnum plicatum* 'Lanarth'. The shrub border contains the National Collection of Lily of the Valley (*Convallaria majalis*).

The Cedar Avenue frames a view of the east front of the house